Cover illustration: Positioned on the waist catapult of the last British conventional aircraft carrier, *Ark Royal*, a Spey-engined Phantom FG.1 of 892 Squadron awaits steam for launch. The Phantom was the most powerful fighter to enter RN service and on the decommissioning of *Ark*, the aircraft were transferred to the RAF for UK air defence duties. (RN via M. H. Larcombe)

1. The front-line service photographic reconnaissance version of the Crusader, known as the RF-8 was withdrawn from service in 1980–1 and replaced by the F-14 Tomcat. Note the cantilever mainplane of these two RF-8A Crusaders aboard *Forrestal* as they prepare for launch from the angle-deck catapults. The photograph was taken in July 1960 and the Crusaders came from VFP-62. In the background, on 'plane guard duties, is a tandem rotor Piasecki HUP Retriever from HU-2. (US Navy)

WARBIRDS ILLUSTRATED NO. 19

Carrier Air Operations

since 1945

PAUL BEAVER

a&ap

ARMS AND ARMOUR PRESS

London – Melbourne – Harrisburg, Pa. – Cape Town

Introduction

Warbirds Illustrated 19: Carrier Air Operations since 1945
Published in 1983 by
Arms and Armour Press, Lionel Leventhal
Limited, 2–6 Hampstead High Street, London
NW3 1QQ; 4–12 Tattersalls Lane, Melbourne,
Victoria 3000, Australia; Sanso Centre, 8 Adderley
Street, P.O. Box 94, Cape Town 8000, South
Africa; Cameron and Kelker Streets, P.O. Box
1831, Harrisburg, Pennsylvania 17105, USA

Layout by Roger Chesneau.
Typesetting and make-up by
Wyvern Typesetting Limited, Bristol.
Printed and bound in Great Britain by
William Clowes, Beccles, Limited.

The aircraft carrier, the floating airfield of the Pacific War, was the undisputed capital ship of the immediate post-war era and was unrivalled until the emergence of the nuclear-powered submarine in the late 1960s. Today, the carrier is expensive to operate and thought by some to be very vulnerable to enemy action. Events in the South Atlantic during the late spring of 1982 proved that *organic* air cover is indispensable to the modern battle commander.

The photographs in this book have been chosen to illustrate the various aspects of aircraft carrier operations on the flight deck, as well as to provide the reader with a view of the changing pattern of carrier aircraft. Although the carrier-borne aircraft has changed since 1945, the basic types will still be recognizable to a naval flyer of that period. The grouping of the photographs is by navies, large and small, with due account being taken of the other books in the Warbirds series. Readers may feel, therefore, that the Argentine, British, American and Soviet naval air arms have not been covered in full, but a complete account of carrier flying was not the purpose of this book.

Paul Beaver, 1983

2. The carrier *Karel Doorman* underwent major reconstruction during her 20 years with the Royal Netherlands Navy, including the provision of modern aids in 1955–8 and again in 1965–6. This picture of a Sea Hawk undergoing maintenance was taken just prior to that conversion; also on deck are an Avenger and the 'plane-guard S-55. *Karel Doorman* was eventually sold to Argentina (and renamed *25 De Mayo*) after a major fire onboard in 1968. (AMH 59229 AVD)

▲3 ▼4

5▲

3. The first Argentine aircraft carrier operated the Chance Vought Corsair piston-engined fighters, which were supplemented with Grumman S-2A Tracker ASW aircraft. The carrier was named *Independencia* (ex-HMS *Warrior*) and served until 1970, being replaced by *25 de Mayo*. Argentine naval forces played a very small part in the Falklands War after the initial invasion of Port Stanley. (Via Adrian English)

4. The S-2 Tracker has been the mainstay of the smaller navies' carrier air groups. This is an S-2E of the Argentine Armada launching from *25 de Mayo* during naval exercises in the Atlantic. The presence of the Alouette III Pedro high above the Tracker serves as a reminder of how dangerous even peacetime carrier operations can be.

5. Australia was one of three Commonwealth countries to benefit from the light fleet aircraft carrier building boom during the last years of the Second World War. *Sydney* (formerly

Terrible) was the first carrier to be transferred, and completed two tours off Korea with the United Nations forces, 1951–53. A firm favourite with Australian pilots was the Hawker Sea Fury which achieved fame over Korea, both as a ground-attack aircraft and in combat against Communist jets. This example was flown from *Sydney* as part of 21 Carrier Air Group. (RN)

6. During the Vietnam War, *Sydney*, no longer classed as an aircraft carrier, having been replaced by the larger *Melbourne*, was recommissioned from the Reserve to serve as a troop and equipment transport. She made twenty voyages to Vietnam in support of the Australian war effort and was known as 'Vung Tau Ferry' by those who sailed in her. Ship-to-shore transportation was provided by Boeing-Vertol CH-47C Chinooks of the Royal Australian Air Force and this picture shows a typical, rotors running, troop transfer underway off the Vietnam coast. (Australian War Memorial SKE 671281)

6▼

▲7 ▼8

7. The close ties between the Royal Navy and her Australian counterpart originally ensured that British aircraft would be purchased for service in Australian carriers. The first helicopters to embark in RAN carriers were the Westland Wessex HAS.31A, as illustrated, which first served in *Sydney* and transferred to *Melbourne* when the latter commissioned. The Mk 31As were later updated to Mk 31B (similar to the RN's HAS.3) to provide anti-submarine warfare (ASW) cover for the carrier and to give over-the-horizon-targeting (OTHT) for Ikara equipped warships of the RAN. (RAN)

8. The first jet of the Royal Australian Navy to go to sea was the DH Sea Venom FAW.53 for all-weather fleet defence and strike. This particular aircraft is seen after deck landing practice aboard *Melbourne* but was normally based ashore at Nowra, with 724 Squadron, RAN. It is quite common for aircraft carriers to be used for DLP by shore-based or training aircraft, especially when only one carrier is available. (Via R. L. Ward)

9. Equipped with long-range tanks and the Billy Pugh rescue net, this RAN Bell UH-1D Iroquois is seen operating in conjunction with *Sydney* during a search and rescue (SAR) exercise off the coast of New South Wales. As a rule, Australian carriers did not carry the Iroquois as part of the embarked air group but used the Wessex as a 'plane guard helicopter during flying operations. Nevertheless, it was common practice to operate short-based helicopters and other aircraft in conjunction with the carriers whenever they were in home waters. (RAN)

9▼

10. The venerable Wessex was replaced in front-line service by the Westland-built Sea King HAS.50 in 1976 but, following several losses at sea, including one during the passage to the 1977 Silver Jubilee Review, another order had to be placed with Westland. The Sea King, which operated with HS-817 Squadron in *Melbourne*, has given the RAN a medium-to-long range ship-borne ASW capability on a par with all other carrier navies. Since this photograph was taken, the Sea Kings have been retro-fitted with FOD (foreign object damage) guards in front of the engine intakes. (RAN)

▲11

11. When the Fairey Gannet AS.1 was retired from RAN service in August 1967, Australia looked to the United States to provide the replacement ASW fixed-wing aircraft for the embarked air group in *Melbourne*. The choice fell on the Grumman S-2E Tracker which was being withdrawn from USN front-line units. The aircraft were overhauled and modified to RAN standards before *Melbourne* sailed to the US west coast to collect them, together with a squadron of McDonnell A-4G Skyhawks. Disaster struck in December 1976 in the shape of a hangar fire which destroyed nine of the S-2Es; these were subsequently replaced by sixteen S-2G Trackers from USN

stocks and one is shown here aboard *Melbourne*. (RAN)

12. The arrival of the McDonnell A-4G Skyhawk meant that the last British-built fleet fighter had been retired from RAN service. The Skyhawk proved a worthy successor to the Sea Venom and gave stalwart service at sea from its introduction with VF805 Squadron in 1967 until the demise of *Melbourne* in 1982. Australian Skyhawks have been equipped with the in-flight refuelling system using the nose probe and budding-pack method as shown in this photograph of a returning A-4G. Note also the bomb racks for the air-to-surface support role. (RAN)

▼12

13. The first of the A-4G Skyhawks arrived in *Melbourne* in 1967 cocooned in protective tape and masking. The aircraft carrier had been completely refitted to modern standards during the period 1963–67 before visiting the United States and Canada. The picture shows an A-4G being swung over the side by crane for transit to RNAS Nowra by catamaran lighter, being incapable of flight; note the USN-style of in-flight refuelling probe and large 300 US gallon fuel tanks on the underwing pylon. The standard armament is two 20mm Mk 12 cannon in the wing root and AIM-9 Sidewinder AAMs. (RAN)

14. One of the final launches of a Skyhawk from the single steam catapult of *Melbourne* during her last operational cruise early in 1982. The carrier, flagship of the Royal Australian Navy, had been in service since 1956, and although refitted and modernized several times, retained the original 40mm Bofors anti-aircraft defence guns. On the flight deck can be seen three other A-4Gs plus one of the two Wessex 'plane guard helicopters; one suspects that this photograph was taken from the cabin of the second, airborne, 'plane guard Wessex. (RAN)

13▲

14▼

▲15

▲16

15. The largest South American nation also operates the largest fleet, and Brazil, like so many maritime nations has long recognized the need for air power at sea. In 1956, the British Admiralty agreed the sale of the former RN/RAN carrier *Vengeance* to Brazil and after re-construction in Rotterdam, the *Minas Gerais* sailed for Rio in 1961. Since then she has operated ASW types, and still flies the Grumman S-2A Tracker, which aircraft are manned by the Air Force. Eight are usually carried, six of which are illustrated here. (Via A. J. Watts)

16. Control of the carrier air element by the Brazilian Air Force has led, sources reveal, to the inflexibility of air operations at sea. Concentration on the ASW role, however, has made the FAB's regular air component in *Minas Gerais* efficient, especially with only one fixed-wing aircraft in service. In Brazilian service, the S-2A Tracker is known as the P-16. The air group is seen here at its shore base in Santa Cruz. (Via Small Air Forces Clearing House)

17. In July 1946, Canada commenced carrier operations when Supermarine Seafires and Fairey Fireflies embarked in the former RN carrier *Warrior* off the coast of Nova Scotia. Despite a temporary grounding of all Seafires because of a supercharger clutch defect, the carrier worked up and operated both in the Atlantic and the Pacific. This view, probably taken in August 1946, shows three Fireflies on deck during training. (DND)

18. The Seafire's replacement was the venerable Hawker Sea Fury, then standard equipment with several fleet air arms around the world. With the new fighters came a new carrier, *Magnificent*, but the Fireflies were retained until replaced by Grumman Avengers. The Sea Fury continued to serve until 1957–58 when the McDonnell Banshee entered service in the RCN's third and last carrier, *Bonaventure*. Many Canadian Sea Furies have been preserved in North America and are used for various recreational pursuits including aerial racing. (RCN)

17▲ 18▼

▲19

19. *Bonaventure* brought a new style of carrier operations to the Canadians with the innovative steam catapult, the angled deck and the mirror deck-landing aid. The carrier saw the arrival of the jet fighter and the twin-engined anti-submarine aircraft. This picture of the carrier steaming off the Atlantic coast of Canada shows a deck park of seven Trackers at Fly One and a single Tracker

▼20

ready for flying. The photograph was taken from the 'plane guard Sikorsky S-55 helicopter. (RCN)

20. The McDonnell F2H-3 (later F2-C) Banshee was operational with the Royal Canadian Navy from 1955 (870 Squadron being the first to receive them) until 1964 when the aircraft was declared obsolescent. The fighter had given sterling service in *Bonaventure*. Its

replacement was to have been the McDonnell-Douglas A-4E Skyhawk and trials were conducted in 1964, but the type was found to be unsuitable, especially after a flying accident during the trials. A Banshee still guards the gate at CFB Shearwater, the former Dartmouth Naval Air Station. (RN)

21. Like all navies, the French have developed the helicopter into a 'jack of all trades'. This view shows an SA316B Alouette III being deck-handled aboard *Arromanches* where the helicopter served as a 'plane guard or 'Pedro'. Other roles have included ASW and surface strike, the Alouette III being one of the most widely used of naval helicopters. During carrier flying operations, the helicopter provides an almost instant rescue service for any personnel, deck or air, who have the misfortune to fall into the 'drink'. (Aérospatiale)

22. Despite the relinquishing of her former empire, France has been conscious of the importance of a global role in peace keeping. In 1957, the French Government authorized the building of a large, 12,360-ton Commando Helicopter Carrier, which could be used as a training ship in peacetime. She can carry eight SA321G Super Frelon Commando/ASW helicopters in wartime, but usually embarks only four for training. A Super Frelon, complete with rescue winch, is seen recovering aboard the ship, commissioned as *Jeanne d'Arc*, in June 1964. (Aérospatiale)

▲23 ▼24

23. Originally purchased as a helicopter carriage, the ex-USN *Dédalo* was transferred to Spain in 1967 for ASW helicopters. In 1976, the Spanish Navy began to supplement the Sikorsky Sea King helicopters with McDonnell Douglas built AV-8A Matadors, five of which are complemented for the ship. Being equipped with Sidewinder missiles, the Matadors' main role is air defence and strike missions against land and sea targets, rather in the same way as the USMC operates its AV-8As.

24. The first true Sea Harrier operator after the Royal Navy is the Indian Navy, whose FRS.51s have relieved the ageing Sea Hawks from the decks of *Vikrant*. Seen here at Farnborough prior to delivery to the Indian Navy Training Flight at Yeovilton, this Sea Harrier is displayed with a full range of armaments, including the BAe Sea Eagle air-launched anti-ship missile which has yet to come into service. It is hoped that after the successful use of the SHA in the Falklands, there will be other orders for this remarkable aircraft. (R. L. Ward)

25. The decision not to replace the jet fighter equipment in *Bonaventure* allowed the embarking of large anti-submarine helicopters to make the carrier an important ASW asset in the NATO inventory. The Trackers remained on board together with the S-55s (known in the RCN as HO4S). This photograph was taken aboard a Canadian destroyer and shows *Bonaventure*'s S-55 'plane guard landing on. (RCN)

26. Bonnie – as *Bonaventure* was known – only rarely voyaged to climates warmer than the North Atlantic or North Sea. She operated off Cyprus and in the West Indies on occasions, but her ASW role (as illustrated) kept her in the Atlantic. The forward deck park holds seven Trackers, while two Sikorsky HSS-2 Sea Kings can be seen on the 'angle' being readied for operations. Right on the stern rounddown is one of the two S-55 'plane guards partly obscuring the ship's hull number, 22. (RCN)

27. The legacy of the carrier aviation of the Royal Canadian Navy has been the Canadian-built Grumman Trackers. *Bonaventure* was prematurely laid up in 1970, only three years after completing a major half-life refit and modernization. Since that date Canada's Armed Forces have been without a large aircraft platform at sea, although their large destroyer design can accommodate two Sea Kings. The Trackers still operate coast surveillance sorties, but are due to be replaced in 1984. (CAF)

25▲

26▲

▲28

▲29

◄30

28. Immediately following the Second World War, the French Navy was reborn into a worldwide – blue water – navy and acquired its first aircraft carriers. Between 1946 and 1951, *Colossus*, a former British light fleet type, was taken on loan, refitted in 1950–51 and renamed *Arromanches*. She served in the colonial wars of South-East Asia and at Suez where she operated Vought AU-1 Corsairs (former US F4U-6 models) of Escadrille 15F. The one illustrated is probably post-Suez; the type served until replaced by the Dassault Etendard in 1962. (Association pour l'Histoire de l'Aéronautique Navale)

29. The heavier strike and anti-submarine role was undertaken by former USN Grumman TBM-3E Avengers, such as this aircraft from Escadrille 5S. During the Algerian conflict, such aircraft operated in support of the Army from shore bases as did many fleet aircraft during the earlier Indo-China War. Among the Avenger aircrew of the 1950s was a certain Lieutenant de vaisseau, Philippe de Gaulle, son of the late President of France. (AHAN).

30. Another variant of the versatile Avenger airframe was the 'eye in the sky' or TBM-3W airborne early warning aircraft. Although only a few were in service with Escadrille 9F, they performed well during their periods afloat in the mid-1950s. The airframe was modified from earlier ASW variants to allow for the carriage of the large American-designed radar radome and to provide accommodation for a radar operator, who could also act as an airborne fighter controller if necessary. (AHAN)

31. The French took an interest in the Royal Navy's De Havilland Sea Venom and produced 60 under licence. Called the Aquilon (north wind), the aircraft were manufactured for the Aéronavale by SNCASE and served in both air defence and ground attack, seeing active service in Algeria. This one is from the first batch of Aquilon 202s of 16F which embarked in *Arromanches* early in 1955; the aircraft served for ten years before being replaced by the Etendard IVP. (Via M. Rostaing/R. L. Ward)

32. The importance of operational training being carried out aboard aircraft carriers has always been recognized by the carrier navies. The French were particularly conscious of this and developed the Fouga Magister into a deck landing trainer. Here, the second example of the CM175 Zephur is being put through its paces aboard *Arromanches* while carrying out trials from its test base at Saint-Raphael, hence the letters SR on the fuselage. Deck landing trials were also carried out aboard the British post-war light fleet carrier *Bulwark* as part of the typical Anglo-French naval co-operation which has been present from the time the Aéronavale flew Supermarine Seafires until the present day. (AHAN)

33. The prototype Breguet Br1050 Alizé (tradewind) first flew in October 1956, so becoming the first French-designed naval aircraft in service in 1959. Basically an anti-submarine aircraft, the Alizé has also been transferred to target facilities and requirement operations over the years. It is still in service with the French and Indian Navies, although the former is seeking a replacement. This is an earlier series Alizé leaving the angled deck of *Clemenceau*, the first French-built post-war aircraft carrier. (AHAN)

31▲

32▲

33▶

34. French marines train regularly for the intervention role which has recently taken troops to Lebanon and previously to various African trouble spots. The Super Frelon can carry approximately 25 marines and the helicopter can then transport them about 200nm (370km) for an assault or opposed landing operation. In its anti-submarine role, the Super Frelon carries sonar gear and four torpedoes, and in the strike role is equipped with the air-launched AM.39 Exocet missile. (Aérospatiale)

35. Throughout the 1960s and 1970s, the standard fleet fighter of the Aéronavale was the Dassault Etendard IV, which was embarked in *Clemenceau* and *Foch* in two versions: the IVM for strike and the IVP for photo-reconnaissance. This rather striking picture of an Etendard IVM, tied back on the steam catapult ready for launch, captures all the thrill of flight deck operations. The aircraft in the background is the replacement Dassault Breguet Super Etendard, a type which sprang to fame in May 1982 when three, in Argentine hands, sank the British destroyer *Sheffield*. The aircraft is transonic and has replaced the units embarked in the two French aircraft carriers of the *Clemenceau* class. (E.C.P. Armées)

▲34 ▼35

36. The all-weather fleet fighter role of the Aéronavale is entrusted to the LTV F-8E(FN) Crusader, 42 of which were delivered by the American builders after modifications to enable them to operate from the relatively small decks of the French *Clemenceau* class carriers. This view shows one of *Foch*'s air group being manoeuvred to the forward lift for transfer to the flight deck. In the background is a rather interesting mixture of Etendard IVP, Alizé and two Fouga Zephyrs (right). The carrier is therefore probably on a training cruise in the Mediterranean. (ECPA)

37. A busy deck scene as the aircraft are re-spotted from the overnight Fly One park to enable flying operations to begin. On the forward lift is a Crusader about to go below, while another tug pulls an Alizé aft. A second is also underway, passing two further Alizé (probably the complete complement), four Etendards and another Crusader. The advantages of folding wings for carrier operations is clearly demonstrated in this photograph from *Clemenceau*. (ECPA)

▲38

38. The hiss of steam and the thunder of a jet exhaust. In Europe, only the French Navy perform fixed-wing carrier operations – the other powers operate either helicopters or STOVL (short take-off and vertical landing) aircraft. The LTV Crusader is due to continue in service until 1990, while the Super Etendard (right) was introduced in 1979 as the tactical fighter for this decade. Both aircraft can easily be operated aboard the *Clemenceau* class until the carriers are phased out of service, although a new airborne early warning aircraft is due to be selected to join them soon; this will mean that the Alizé will be superseded by helicopters almost completely. (ECPA)

39. *Foch* at flying stations. This view shows an Alizé about to recover on the deck, watched over by the Alouette III Pedro. The embarked air group consists of Etendard, Crusader and Alizé, which would date the photograph to 1979. For economy, it is envisaged that *Foch* will operate helicopters only, during peacetime operations, when her sister-ship *Clemenceau* is at sea. *Foch* is, therefore, being geared to anti-submarine work in support of the French strategic deterrent force of nuclear-powered ballistic missile submarines. (ECPA)

▼39

40▲

41▲

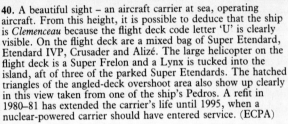

40. A beautiful sight – an aircraft carrier at sea, operating aircraft. From this height, it is possible to deduce that the ship is *Clemenceau* because the flight deck code letter 'U' is clearly visible. On the flight deck are a mixed bag of Super Etendard, Etendard IVP, Crusader and Alizé. The large helicopter on the flight deck is a Super Frelon and a Lynx is tucked into the island, aft of three of the parked Super Etendards. The hatched triangles of the angled-deck overshoot area also show up clearly in this view taken from one of the ship's Pedros. A refit in 1980–81 has extended the carrier's life until 1995, when a nuclear-powered carrier should have entered service. (ECPA)

41. Another mixed bag is illustrated in this view from the 'plane guard helicopter. The forward deck park – Fly One – has most of the fixed-wing air group embarked, including no less than thirteen Super Etendards and a Crusader, while two Alouette III's are parked on the angle. Moving aft, past the relatively small island of *Clemenceau*, the fourteenth Super Etendard is parked by the deck edge lift, a Crusader is being moved to the waist catapult and two Alizés are ready to be towed away. Again this view would seem to indicate the beginning of a day's flying operations, although the Westland Lynx HAS.2(FN) with its main rotors being folded is an unusual visitor to an aircraft carrier, the type usually operating from frigates and destroyers. (ECPA)

▲42

42. When India joined the carrier club in 1961 with the commissioning of the British light fleet type, *Vikrant* (ex-*Hercules*), the Hawker Sea Hawk fighter was just leaving Royal Naval service. The Indian Navy purchased twenty former RN aircraft from surplus stocks of FGA.6s. They were delivered to India in 1960 to commence trials prior to embarking in the new carrier. This rare photograph shows a flight of four off the British coast prior to delivery. (Ray Williams)

▼43

43. It is even more rare to find pictures of Indian naval aircraft operating at sea. This is a delightful shot of a Sea Hawk FGA.6 in *Vikrant*, about to be launched from the steam catapult. The letter 'W' on the tail of the aircraft identifies it as coming from the carrier, but unfortunately, the sun has obscured the leaping tiger unit badge on the nose. The Sea Hawk has only recently been phased out of service, being replaced by the British Aerospace Sea Harrier. (Via Ray Williams)

44▲

44. The early post-war naval aviation of the Netherlands followed British lines, and included the acquisition of two British-built carriers, both renamed *Karel Doorman*, and aircraft. Like the RN's light fleet carriers, the Dutch operated a mixed air group of Hawker Sea Furies and Fairey Fireflies. Shown here is a Firefly FRIV about to launch from *Karel Doorman* (II) during a visit to the Dutch West Indies. (Afdeling Maritieme Historie 521–11)

45. Operating in the western Atlantic with a new colour scheme of dark sea-grey and blue-grey, this US-built Avenger is seen after recovery taxiing to be spotted forward. Note the wings have powered folding and the clean appearance of the aircraft. (AMH 59233 AVD)

45▼

46–49. The scenes here illustrate problems which could be encountered with carrier operations even on calm days. The leader of the Dutch Avenger unit took his aircraft and crews to *Bulwark* for deck landing practice in October 1955, but had a slight problem returning ashore. At about half the recommended take-off speed the 'Guppy' developed an uncontrollable swing to starboard and stalled into the sea. The carrier's plane-guard Dragonfly was soon on the scene, however, and recovered the crew via the Sproule rescue net. (Commander R. H. Kilburn via FAAOA)

◀ 46–49

50. The RN's light fleet carrier *Venerable* became *Karel Doorman* (II). After a major refit in 1954, she embarked her first jets: like India, the Royal Netherlands Navy purchased, via NATO funding, about 30 Hawker Sea Hawk FGA.50s for the fleet fighter role. Major items in the refit were the installation of an angled deck and a steam catapult system, and this Sea Hawk of 860 Squadron is putting the latter to good use on a grey Atlantic day. Note the large number of flight deck personnel involved in the launch of the older style aircraft and compare this view to others of more modern times elsewhere in the book. When the carrier was rated for anti-submarine warfare, the Sea Hawks were withdrawn from service and replaced by Sikorsky H-34 Seabat helicopters. (Via Ray Williams)

51. This photograph gives a vivid impression of the rather startling engine starting procedure used by the Sea Hawk. The smoke is caused by cartridge starters igniting and there is no danger to the aircraft or crew. (Via Ray Williams)

▲52 ▼53

54▲

52. The well-named 'badgers' watch the launch of a Dutch Seahawk FGA.50 aboard *Karel Doorman*, while the 'plane-guard Whirlwind (Sikorsky S-55 type) with door open and diver at the ready hovers off the port beam. This view was probably taken during an Atlantic deployment to the West Indies, a regular haunt of the Dutch Navy. (AMH 59038 AVD)

53. The final fixed-wing ASW aircraft to see service afloat with the Dutch Navy were the Grumman S2F-1 (S-2A) Trackers which, with Sikorsky Seabats, eventually formed the final air group of *Karel Doorman*. This Tracker is nicely set to take the arrester wires, monitored by the LSO (Landing Safety Officer) and his assistant on their 'perch' at the first wire. The Tracker later served ashore on maritime patrol duties and later as a target tug, leaving service in the mid-1970s. (AMH 611786 AVD)

54. Seen away from its normal habitat, this Sikorsky SH-34J (HSS-1N) Seabat was the last carrier-borne helicopter to be acquired by the Dutch Navy and it served afloat until 1968. Six Seabats served aboard *Karel Doorman* with 8 Squadron where they operated as 'plane-guards and, equipped with dipping sonar, as ASW components. (F. J. Bachofner)

▲55 ▼56

▼57

55. In addition to the five Matadors, the normal air group in *Dédalo* includes two TAV-8As for continuation training. This line-up of Matadors and a TAV-8A illustrates well the colour scheme of the aircraft in Spanish service. The flight deck markings are strikingly red/yellow. The AV-8A could well be replaced by the AV-8B, Harrier II, in the next five years, but in the meantime the aircraft provides valuable organic air cover to the Spanish Armada.

56. The Agusta AB212ASW helicopter is often seen in company with *Dédalo*, and can operate as a 'plane-guard although this is perhaps a waste of such a valuable ASW asset.

57. The use of Matadors on the wooden deck of the Spanish carrier *Dédalo* must have caused some difficulties when the first operations began, but no serious problems have been reported. The Spanish Navy uses a destroyer in the 'plane guard role, but occasionally helicopters are also seen. This Matador is returning from a training flight without armament.

58. Many of the aircraft developed for the Pacific War did not arrive in service until after peace had been declared. The De Havilland Sea Hornet was no exception, going to sea in 1949. This is one of the early Sea Hornet F.20s recovering aboard HMS *Implacable* where it served until replaced by the Sea Fury two years later. Although not long in service, it was described as his favourite aeroplane by the famous naval test pilot, Captain Eric Brown. (RN)

59. The Hawker Sea Fury was a pilot's aeroplane in every detail. Apart from being the first RN aircraft to destroy a jet in combat, in Korea in 1952, the Sea Fury devastated the North Korean infrastructure during rocket raids (like this one) on enemy transport and positions during 1951–53. Almost immediately after the conflict, however, the aircraft was superseded by jet types, notably the Hawker Sea Hawk. The RN's last piston-engined fleet fighter, the Sea Fury also served in the Royal Australian, Royal Canadian and Royal Netherlands Navies. (RN).

59▼

▲60

▲61 ▼62

60. The Sea Fury's stable-mate was the Fairey Firefly, which had been developed during the War as a long-range fleet reconnaissance fighter. The newer, post-war variants were designed for ASW and strike operations, flying operational sorties in Korea and Malaya during the late 1940s and early 1950s. These Firefly AS.5s are seen making accelerator-assisted launches from HMS *Vengeance* in about 1948. (RN)

61. The helicopter began to appear on carrier decks in 1950, but it was during the Korean War that the RN really became interested in rotary-wing flying. During the early stages of the conflict, the RN were lent several Sikorsky S-51s (later to be built in the UK as Dragonflies) for 'plane-guard duties. This example, being viewed with great interest aboard *Theseus* in 1951, was the helicopter complement of the US flagship *Rochester* in Korean waters. (Courtesy Rear Admiral Bolt)

62. The Sea Fury FB.11 equipped all but one of the Korean fighter units, including those aboard the Australian carrier *Sydney*. This very crowded flight deck park illustrates the number of aircraft carried by carriers during the period. Aboard *Theseus* in this picture is almost the whole of 807 Squadron, part of the 17th Carrier Air Group. Note the black and white Korean 'stripes' on the Furies' wings and fuselages. (Courtesy Rear Admiral Bolt)

63. The halcyon days of the British fixed-wing carrier were in the early 1960s, when this photograph of *Hermes* was taken off Gibraltar. The carrier is on her way back to England after a Mediterranean exercise and has a deck range of four Gannet AEW.3s from 849 Squadron, plus, in very distinctive red and navy-blue SAR colours, a Westland Whirlwind HAR.9. A fifth Gannet can be seen on the rounddown. (RN via M. H. Larcombe)

64. With Supermarine Scimitars of 803 Squadron gracing her deck, the last commissioned British fixed-wing carrier, *Hermes* begins another day's flying in the Atlantic. The other aircraft ranged on deck are Sea Vixens, which complemented the Scimitar well while in service. (RN via M. H. Larcombe)

▲65

65. Only the British, it was said, could develop a heavy and powerful strike aircraft and still keep it subsonic, but it was this very facet of its performance which enabled it to cope with the task it was designed to fulfil. If the Blackburn (later Hawker Siddeley) Buccaneer had been stressed for supersonic flight, it would not have been the naval aircraft it turned out to be. Like the Phantoms which made up the last strike air group in *Ark Royal*, the RN's Buccaneers were transferred to the RAF in 1978, and are still flying. (RN via M. H. Larcombe)

66. The Sea Vixen was the last British fixed-wing conventional fighter to serve afloat. A pilot's dream but an observer's curse, the Sea Vixen, nevertheless, gave the Fleet Air Arm an aircraft which could operate on equal terms with those of land-based forces. The type formed the key element in *Eagle*'s last air

group and was flying throughout the period of confrontation in Indonesia and during the Beira Patrol. Shown here is a Sea Vixen FAW.1 'bolting' from the deck of *Hermes* in 1962 or 1963. (RN via M. H. Larcombe)

67. The climax of the Fleet Air Arm's fixed-wing strength at sea was the aircraft carrier *Ark Royal* and her last air group which comprised American-built but British-engined McDonnell Douglas F-4K Phantoms, Hawker Siddeley Buccaneer S.2s and the Fairey-Westland Gannet AEW.3 airborne early warning aircraft. In effect, the carrier air group thus composed represented one of the best equipped 'air forces' in the world. It was not until the Falklands conflict that the Royal Navy realized how much they need airborne early warning. (RN via M. H. Larcombe)

▼66

67▶

68. During the Vietnam War, the chunky LTV A-7 Corsair served with the US forces both ashore and afloat, and its powerful performance and good load-carrying proved equal to the rigours of action in South-East Asia. These two A-7As are seen with an F-8 Crusader (left), an aircraft with which they are often confused, and which occasionally formed the air defence element of USN carrier air groups off Vietnam. (Via R. L. Ward)

69. *Ranger's* flight deck is ready to receive aircraft as a flight of five Corsair IIs orbit, hooks down, to recover. The aircraft are carrying varying warloads of rocket pods and two or more Sidewinder air-to-air missiles. The aircraft on deck, part of the carrier's air group while operating with the Seventh Fleet, include four F-4 Phantoms, two RA-5C Vigilantes, three EA-3 Skywarriors, a single E-2 Hawkeye, a single A-6A Intruder and a lone A-4 Skyhawk. The common mix for the *Forrestal* class at this time would be two fighter squadrons, two or three attack units, a flight of AEW aircraft and one or two flights of reconnaissance types. The ship's flight of 'plane guard helicopters were usually not included in the air group make-up. (Via R. L. Ward)

70. Typical of the mid-50s air groups in British carriers were the Sea Hawk (foreground – from 898 Squadron), Westland Wyverns (831 Squadron), Gannet AS.4 (815 Squadron) and two of 849 B Flight's Douglas Skyraider airborne early warning aircraft. This scene was photographed aboard *Ark Royal* during her second commission. (RN)

71. *Ark Royal* again – this time during a review by HM The Queen in Moray Firth. The nearest Hawker Sea Hawk FGA.6 bears the tiger and blade motif of 804 Squadron. Eagle-eyed readers will be able to detect Sea Hawk 470 from 898 Squadron in the line-up on the port side of the flight deck; this aircraft still flies with the Fleet Air Arm Historic Flight. (Courtesy Admiral Hopkins)

70▲ 71▼

▲▶72,73

▲▶74,75

72. In the 1950s
and early 1960s there were
a number of particularly bad accidents
on the small flight decks of British light fleet
carriers. Fortunately, few of them (including this one) resulted
in major loss of life, unlike the accidents which bedevilled the USN off
Vietnam. Aboard *Centaur*, Sea Hawk 150 has a throttle jam and careers headlong for
the deck park – 148 is also taxiing in. **73.** Sea Hawk 150 hits 148 and the other parked Hawks
while flight deck personnel take cover – several in fact, jump overboard and are rescued by the 'plane guard
Dragonfly. **74.** The tail of Sea Hawk 150 breaks off and the fuselage and wings are about to go over the side. Note the
flight deck and aircrews running to assist the injured. **75.** The aftermath is one Sea Hawk totally destroyed and over the side
(just its tail remaining on deck), another very badly damaged, plus three damaged but reparable.

▲76

76. The Sea Hawk's partner was the De Havilland Sea Venom, a naval fighter which gave the first semblance of all-weather performance to the Fleet Air Arm. Seen here aboard *Eagle*, a Sea Venom FAW.22 of 894 Squadron taxies to the steam catapult. Alongside is one of *Eagle*'s two Westland Whirlwind HAR.7 'plane-guard helicopters. The Sea Venom remained in fleet service until 1960, while the Whirlwind 7 retained both ASW and Commando roles until the early 1970s. (RN)

▼77

77. Cross-deck operations were an important part of the training of early jet operators at sea as shown by this Banshee making a touch-and-go circuit of *Eagle*'s flight deck. Parked to starboard is part of the resident air group's Sea Hawk complement. When this photograph was taken in 1955, *Eagle* was in company with USS *Coral Sea* in the Mediterranean. (Courtesy Captain Lewin)

78. The Westland Wyverns S.4 was one of the interesting British post-war innovatory designs, including ejection seat and contra-rotating eight-bladed propellers. Four front-line units were equipped with the type and they successfully took their aircraft to *Albion*, *Ark Royal* and *Eagle*. During the Suez operation, two Wyverns were lost and one pilot completed what is thought to have been the first RN ejection after combat. (RN)

79. The Egyptian annexation of the Suez Canal led to Anglo-French intervention in November 1956. The RN sent *Albion*, *Bulwark* and *Eagle* to the area to provide air cover for the landing force. The Sea Hawks, Wyverns and Sea Venoms (illustrated) were highly successful, and from a purely naval point of view the operation, codenamed 'Musketeer', was also highly successful. Here pilots of 809 Squadron have just returned from a strike against Almaza. (Courtesy R. B. Wigg)

82. The hazards of normal flight deck flying are amply illustrated in this series of photographs taken aboard *Hermes* during her 1963–4 commission in the Mediterranean. The Scimitar, from 803 Squadron, has failed to take the last arrester wire and the safety barrier has been raised to prevent the aircraft from crashing into the sea. **83.** The barrier slows the Scimitar down, breaking one of the wing drop tanks in the process. **84.** Finally stationary, the Scimitar is immediately surrounded by the crash crew who can be seen swabbing the deck with sea water where the drop tank has leaked. Using the fork-lift truck, the rescue crew are extracting the pilot. (Courtesy Admiral O'Brien)

▼ 82, 83, 84

80. Flight deck operations can be hazardous at any time, and the breaking of waves over the bow of the carrier does not help personnel to keep their footing or contribute to the serviceability of the parked aircraft. Aboard *Hermes*, these Scimitar F.1 of 803 Squadron are receiving the full force of the Atlantic, while the flight deck crew clear a Gannet AEW.3 of 849B Flight for launch. (Courtesy Admiral O'Brien)
81. The Supermarine Scimitar F.1 was the last British-built conventional fleet strike fighter and served in four front-line squadrons aboard most of the large carriers, including *Ark Royal* (illustrated here with an 800 Squadron aircraft over the rounddown). The *modus operandi* of landing the Scimitar has been likened by some pilots to that of a controlled crash, but the fighter was a worthy asset to the fleet during the early 1960s. (Courtesy Vice-Admiral Gibson)

◀80   81▶

45

85. Embarked in *Hermes* in 1962 were De Havilland Sea Vixen FAW.1s of 892 Squadron. The carrier was used the same year for Sea Vixen FAW.2 trials, the first updated model arriving in service in 1963. The Vixen, loved by pilots but not so popular with the observer who resided in the 'coal hole' of the fuselage, was a good carrier all-weather fighter and remained in service until 1972. (RN)

86. When 801 Squadron embarked in *Ark Royal* in February 1963 with their new Blackburn Buccaneer S.1, the RN had received its first truly nuclear-capable strike fighter. The two-man crew and complex avionics made the Buccaneer a formidable aircraft, but its weight made it rather difficult to operate at sea. The all-white colour scheme of this Buccaneer was in keeping with the RAF's V-Bomber force of the time. (RN)

▲85 ▼86

87. *Hermes* spent a good deal of her time in the Indian Ocean and Mediterranean, especially during the troublesome 1960s. Regular cross-decking operations were mounted with the USN. Here USS *Ranger*'s HUP helicopter approaches the flight deck during helicopter operations; on deck are Gannets, Sea Vixens and a Scimitar, with an 814 Squadron Wessex HAS.1 in the centre of the angle. (Courtesy Admiral O'Brien)

88. USS *Independence* sent across F-4J Phantom IIs of VF-102, including the squadron commander, when she met *Ark Royal* in mid Atlantic in 1975. The *Ark* was also operating Phantoms at that time; her flight deck was strong enough to withstand the extra heat generated at take-off. (RN)

▲89

89. Airborne – an LTV F-8 Crusader lifts away from *Ark Royal* to return to *Independence* after a cross-deck visit. (RN)

90. Helicopters aboard carriers are used mainly for ASW, and for air commando support as illustrated here by Wessex HAR.1 helicopters from the converted commando-carrier *Albion*. The Wessex are painted in the sand and spinach scheme of the Middle East (Aden) and the Far East (Borneo), two areas where they were kept busy during the 1960s. (RN)

91. The risks of ditching are always high in carrier aviation, whether in peace or war. The RN's answer to this problem was to use 'plane-guard helicopters with trained SAR divers who could be dropped directly on to the crash scene. In this exercise, an SAR diver is being dropped from a Whirlwind HAR.7 of *Ark Royal*'s rescue flight. (RN)

◀90 91▼

92. The final commission of *Ark Royal*, following her equipping with Phantoms, saw the last use of British fixed-wing conventional naval fighters. With the cancellation of the P.1154 project, the perhaps better alternative of the American-built but British-equipped F-4K Phantom II was adopted and these aircraft joined 892 Squadron in *Ark Royal* in 1970. The interesting nose markings were originally intended for the 1977 Silver Jubilee Review, and were later revised for the final year of commission. (Fleet Photographic Unit)

93. With the demise of the fixed-wing carrier, the RN still operate the ASV/Commando carriers *Bulwark* and *Hermes*. Pictured off Scotland in May 1979 is a visiting Sea King HAR.3 of the RAF's Search and Rescue Unit, undergoing RN training. In the background is a Sea King HAS.2 of 826 Squadron, the resident ASW unit in *Bulwark*. (HMS *Bulwark*)

▲94

▼97

94–97. Although the British carrier fleet was declining, training in all aspects of carrier aviation continued. In 1975, a flight deck safety film was shot aboard *Ark Royal* which necessitated the ditching of an old Buccaneer S.1 airframe over the stern. The aircraft had been stripped of most of its gear, with just enough being left to afford a degree of realism. These dramatic pictures show the sort of problems faced by SAR crews in attempting rescues. Fortunately, by the end of her service career *Ark* had had a very good safety record, and no ditchings had occurred. (Fleet Photographic Unit)

▲98

98. Although in 1966 it was decided to disband the RN's carrier forces, development of the light aircraft carrier (or through-deck cruiser as it was known then) went ahead, and later the navalized Harrier was added to the design. In 1981 *Invincible*, the first of the new class, embarked the second operational Sea Harrier Squadron (801) for trials. Both ship and squadron fought in the

Falklands campaign and proved themselves a very effective unit. (Stephen Wolf)

99. *Illustrious*, the second ship of the *Invincible* class, was completed by her builders in record time to relieve *Invincible* in the Falklands. Seen here entering the American port of Fort Lauderdale on her way home from the South Atlantic, *Illustrious* has ranged on

deck nine Sea Harrier FRS.1s, eight Westland Sea King HAS.5s and a single Wessex HAR.5 'plane-guard helicopter. Several of this air group had been transferred at sea from *Invincible* at the beginning of her deployment. (RN/HMS *Heron*)

▼99

100. The F-14A Tomcat is probably the most powerful fleet fighter anywhere in the world, being armed with the Phoenix AAM, guided by the AWG-9 missile control system. It was 'blooded' in combat with Libyan Su-22 swing-wing fighters over the Mediterranean, when two F-14s from *Nimitz* shot down two attacking aircraft. Using the TARPS reconnaissance pod, the aircraft will be used for tactical, high-speed recce for fleet purposes. (D. G. White)

101. The heaviest carrier-borne aircraft currently in service, the EA-3B Skywarrior has been in fleet service since 1960, having been initially developed as a nuclear-capable bomber and later modified to be an airborne tanker. The aircraft's exact role is surrounded by secrecy but is known to involve both shore-based and carrier-based sorties with a crew of two pilots and four/five electronic systems specialists. (D. G. White)

▲102 ▼103

102. The USN's spy in the sky is the E-2C Hawkeye airborne early warning aircraft which has also been considered for French naval service. The problems of stowing such a large aircraft have been partly overcome by its ability to fold down, and it can taxi around the flight deck with main wings folded back. This example comes from Squadron VAW-126, photographed in the Mediterranean in 1980. (D. G. White)
103. The early morning sky provides the backdrop for this portrait of the returning E-2C Hawkeye sortie, seen landing between parked F-14A Tomcats and S-3A Viking ASW jets aboard USS *John F. Kennedy*. The equipment of modern US naval aircraft carriers makes them mini air forces, many times more powerful than the bulk of the world's air arms. (D. G. White)

104. An idea of what flight deck operations are like in the South Atlantic is given in this view of *Illustrious*'s flight deck, with a Sea Harrier FRS.1 from 809 Squadron at readiness, another available, and an ECM-equipped Sea King HAS.5 of 814 Squadron in the foreground. The snowy scene is reminiscent of Korea or the Arctic convoys. Although the British conventional carrier-borne aircraft story has ended, the use of CVLs with STOVL aircraft, like the Sea Harrier, will continue and three carriers will remain in service for the rest of the decade. (RN/HMS *Heron*)

104▼

▲105

105. Immediately after the Second World War, the US Navy began working with Grumman to develop a jet-powered night fighter for carrier use, initially using British engines, but later those manufactured under licence by Pratt & Whitney. The design was christened Panther by the constructors and designated F9F by the Navy. Entering service in 1949, the type was operational in time for Korea where it achieved notable successes including the first US Navy kills. This F9F-2, apparently a development aircraft, is dumping fuel from tip tanks. (Via R. L. Ward)

106. The Panther fighter-bomber was truly at home over the sea where it served with front-line units until 1954, being then put ashore to operate with reserve units, until finally leaving the US Navy in 1958 after several years with VAH-7 Squadron. The design was important in the future development of the naval fighter-bomber or strike aircraft, having proved the viability of such deployment by an attack on a railway bridge in North Korea in April 1951, thus paving the way for the use of carrier-borne air power against land targets. (Via R. L. Ward)

107. The US Navy took steps to counter the growing submarine threat by developing a torpedo-bomber into a dedicated anti-submarine aircraft. The 274kt (507kmph) Grumman AF-2 Guardian served ashore and afloat from October 1950 until August 1955 in both 'hunter' (AS-2W) and 'killer' (AF-2S) roles. An example of the latter is illustrated, from VS-36 Squadron. (US Navy)

108. During the Falklands conflict the major carrier-borne strike aircraft of the Argentine Navy (ARA) was the Douglas A-4 Skyhawk. The first Skyhawk flew in 1954 and the type entered service in 1956; the A-4B (which the ARA used as the A-4Q in their attacks on the Royal Navy) first flew in 1956 and production continued until the late 1950s. The design has seen service in Vietnam and the Middle East, being likely to remain in service until the late 1980s. Despite the presence of Skyraiders, this A-4F Skyhawk (VA-83) is actually aboard *Hermes* during cross-deck operations with USS *Enterprise* in 1962.

▼106

107▼

108▼

▲109 ▼110

111▲

109. Following the success of the Guardian, the US Navy and Grumman considered putting both roles – hunter and killer – into one anti-submarine platform for carrier use. The design also called for good range and twin-engine safety. The result was the Grumman S2F Tracker which for the last three decades has been the most important fixed-wing ASW aircraft afloat. This S2F-1 is at full power, the carrier's catapult officer (left) having just given the launch signal for the steam catapult to throw the Tracker into the air. Note that the upper cabin hatch is open to provide a rapid means of escape should this 13-ton aeroplane fail to become airborne. (US Navy)

110. Of all the carrier fighters of the 1950s, the Grumman F11F Tiger was surely the most elegant and most futuristic. Designed as a fleet fighter for air superiority over the carrier and the target area, it was developed from the straight-wing Panther and the swept-wing Cougar. It first flew in 1954, but production and test-flying problems delayed its entry into service. The Tiger became operational with VA-156 Squadron in March 1957, but only remained in service until 1961. Cleared for launch is an F11F-1, probably during test flying in *Saratoga* because none of the five operational Tiger units ever served aboard as part of the Air Group. (Grumman)

111. Developed from the basic Tracker design, the E-1B Tracer was the first major attempt to put a good airborne early warning (AEW) radar into the air on a stable platform in a purpose-designed airframe. The earlier attempts using Skyraiders and Avengers were fine during the interim, but USN policies required an aircraft with longer range. The radar used was the APS-82 with 360° cover and housed in the lens-shaped radome above the fuselage. Unlike later AEW aircraft, the radome did not rotate. This Tracer is ready for launch aboard USS *Franklin D. Roosevelt* in September 1966. (USN/PHC Crowe)

◀112
113▲

112. The 15-ton Chance Vought F-8 Crusader is a large aircraft by any standards, yet it was the first US naval aircraft to attain supersonic speed in level flight and thus became the US Navy's standard day fighter from 1957 until 1962. Designed to carry missiles and cannon, the Crusader was soon developed to carry out all-weather fleet fighter roles, and later strike missions. It served in Vietnam and with both the Atlantic and Pacific Fleets, as well as with the Aéronavale where it is still the fleet fighter. Both USN and USMC squadrons operated the aircraft afloat, but these examples aboard *Forrestal* in the Atlantic are from Squadron VF-62 which is no longer in commission (Via R. L. Ward)

113. In this classically posed view of 'plane and carrier, one of *Forrestal*'s FR-8A Crusaders (VFP-62) flies in the landing pattern somewhere off the Atlantic coast of the USA. The Crusader's camera pack can be seen beneath the US insignia, and these were carried in place of guns. In 1962, these aircraft played a major part in the day and night surveillance of Soviet ships during the Cuban missile crisis, although *Forrestal* herself was not involved. The carrier went on to serve off Vietnam and is currently undergoing a major refit to prepare her for another decade's service. (Chance Vought)

114. A design of the early 1960s, the LTV A-7 Corsair II was still in production more than a decade later, albeit for land-based operations. Basically, the US Navy required an airframe with better load-carrying performance than the Skyhawk, but with the robustness of the Crusader. The Corsair II first flew in September 1965, entered service in October 1966 and was in action by December 1967 over the paddy-fields of Vietnam. Important features of the design to note from this view, taken aboard USS *America* during Carrier Qualifications in November 1966, are the catapult slide being positioned and the discrete inflight refuelling probe below the cockpit. (US Navy)

114▼

▲115

115. A good example of American cross-decking with an LTV A-7A Corsair II from Squadron VA-82 (USS *America*) about to launch from USS *Coral Sea* during fighter-bomber attacks on Vietnamese targets by US Seventh Fleet units in the spring of 1968. Besides the two nose Colt Mk 12 20mm cannon, the Corsair II could lift 15,000lb (6,804kg) of bombs on underwing and fuselage pylons, which made the aircraft a useful tool in the air war over South-East Asia. A-7s of various Marks flew more than 100,000 operational sorties between 1967 and 1975. (US Navy)

116. USS *Coral Sea* of the *Midway* class was a Second World War design of the large aircraft carrier type (CVB), although during the course of the Korean War she was re-designated an attack carrier (CVA), before being again re-designated, this time to that of multi-mission carrier (CV). Surprisingly, she has remained in full commission for several years after her

projected end of service date and has been modernized to operate such new types as the Grumman E-2 Hawkeye. This AEW aircraft, with a large, spinning radar radome mounted above the fuselage, must be the most easily recognizable naval aircraft ever designed. (Via R. L. Ward)

117. The Corsair II made its debut from the fleet carrier USS *Ranger* in December 1967 when Squadron VA-147 – the 'Argonauts' – took their new birds to the Gulf of Tonkin at a time when the US Seventh Fleet kept at least one aircraft carrier within strike range of Vietnam. This rather war-weary A-7A is carrying rocket pods and two early-model Sidewinders on fuselage racks while overflying its parent carrier, *Ranger*. Note the latter's 'plane guard or 'goalkeeper' destroyer at the very top of the picture and the assorted aircraft on deck, including Phantom, Skyhawk, Skywarrior and Vigilante jets. (US Navy)

▼116

117▶

▲118 ▼119

118. *JFK*, in common with most of the multi-mission carriers, has an air group of fighters (two squadrons), attack aircraft (three), anti-submarine aircraft (two), ECM (one) plus a flight of AEW and special operations aircraft as required. Having recovered aboard *Kennedy* this A-7E Corsair II from Squadron VA-72 'Blue Hawks' is clearing the deck. The port underwing tank is for inflight refuelling. (D. G. White)

119. A packed flight deck after early morning rain in the Mediterranean as an E-2C Hawkeye from Squadron VAW-126 is the first aircraft of the day to be launched – the time is approximately 0530 and flying is due to last all day. The aircraft ranged on the starboard side are Grumman A-6E Intruders and Grumman EA-6B Prowlers (tandem cockpits). The Intruder is both an attack and tanker aircraft, while the Prowler, which was developed from the Intruder, is an advanced electronics countermeasures (ECM) and Intelligence-gathering (ELINT) aircraft. The flight scene was captured aboard *John F. Kennedy*, the last of the conventionally powered US aircraft carriers to be built. (D. G. White)

120. ASW is a major part of the modern fixed-wing aircraft carriers' daily work. Aboard USN carriers, the fixed-wing task rests on the shoulders of the advanced, twin-jet Lockheed S-3A Viking, shown here taxiing and unfolding its wings prior to launch. The aircraft entered service in 1975 and the last of 187 ordered for the Fleet was delivered in 1978. There were studies to develop an electronic surveillance version, but the cost would be high, and perhaps out of reach of even the USN. Although it has not been operated in anger, the Viking's war load is impressive, including Mk 46 ASW torpedoes, Mk 82 depth-bombs and mines internally, while the wing hard points can take missiles, rockets, bombs or overload fuel tanks. (D. G. White)

▲121 ▼122

121. The modern aircraft carrier at sea is a majestic and powerful sight. In this view of *John F. Kennedy* deployed with the US Sixth Fleet, in the Mediterranean, the combined might of the aircraft parked on deck is greater than that of many of the world's air forces. The aircraft carrier is an ideal way of projecting foreign policy as the US has found since 1945, and as the Soviets are obviously discovering as they build their first fixed-wing carriers. Carriers like *JFK* can accommodate about 85 aircraft and displace 82,000 tons when loaded. (US Navy)

122. When it entered service in 1974, the Grumman F-14A Tomcat was thought to be the greatest fighter available; it is still considered so today. The reason for this is the aircraft's performance and the incredible AIM-54 Phoenix missile for the defence of the carrier task force against Soviet long-range supersonic bombers. This F-14A is aboard *Kennedy* and serves with CVW-1 (Carrier Air Wing One) in one of the two fighter squadrons; this unit is VF-32 'Swordsmen'. Note the elevator angle as the steam rises for launch. (D. G. White)

68

123. Moving away down the port main catapult (one of four) in *JFK*, the F-14A uses her afterburners for the required power to lift a 26-ton jet fighter off the deck. Another's smoke trail can be seen in the sky above her. The structure immediately behind the catapult is the blast deflector shield, which prevents damage to other aircraft and personnel on the flight deck during a launch. About to work-up steam on the starboard catapult is an S-3A Viking, while behind waits an EA-6B Prowler. (D. G. White)

124. Visiting *JFK* in the Mediterranean is a Kaman SH-2F LAMPS-I Seasprite helicopter from a light helicopter anti-submarine squadron (HSL-34 – the 'Green Checkers'). Helicopters deployed in cruisers, destroyers and frigates often visit other ships and several aircraft of this type have been used for search and rescue duties aboard carriers in the past. (D. G. White)

123▲ 124▼

125. Anchored at Spithead, off Portsmouth, the CVN *Dwight D. Eisenhower* has the distinctive silhouette, of the USN CVNs. The open hangar deck can be seen under the after lift and careful inspection will show the tail of an S-3A Viking. Overhead an SH-3D Sea King prepares to recover on the angle deck. (RN)

▲126

126. In toned down grey is this F-14A Tomcat with the tail code 'AG' indicating that it is from an Atlantic Ocean-based carrier – in fact from *Eisenhower* during a NATO/Sixth Fleet cruise. The main armament of the F-14A is the M61A Vulcan cannon (muzzle seen below the aircraft's number 114) while Sidewinder, Sparrow and/or Phoenix missiles are carried in the fuselage or on the wing pylons. This plane is currently the ultimate in carrier-borne aircraft. (RN)

127. Poised sixty feet above sea level, the deck park of the nuclear-powered aircraft carrier *Dwight D. Eisenhower* is akin to a scrap-yard when the carrier is in port. The hangar decks are usually cleared of all aircraft to provide accommodation for entertaining guests. The flight deck's angle is used as a heli-pad as here with the Sikorsky SH-3D Sea King from HS-6. Some of the aircraft are wearing the normal peacetime colour scheme, others the toned down light grey which is becoming a vogue among the navies of the world. In this picture only 50 per cent of the normal air complement is visible! (RN)

►125

128. The emergence of the Soviet Union as a naval aviation power with aircraft carriers is taken to be one of the most serious developments for NATO in the maritime sphere since the nuclear submarine was introduced. The 37,000-ton *Kiev* class has allowed the Soviets to put fixed-wing aircraft to sea for the first time. The aircraft shown is the Yak-36 Forger, a VSTOL fighter which was first pictured at sea in 1976 by the RN. The Forger is less capable than modern NATO counterparts, but it does indicate the way Soviet naval aviation is going, and another type will probably be in service soon. (RN)

129. The *Kiev* class currently consists of *Kiev* and *Minsk* with a third carrier undergoing trials in the Baltic Sea. It is widely reported that the Soviets will also continue to develop their nuclear-power programme and a new super-carrier with this type of propulsion is expected by 1985. She will also be equipped with fixed-wing aircraft such as Forger, but also with Kamov Ka-25 Hormone helicopters (as seen on deck) and Ka-32 Helix types under development (RAF)

▲128   ▼129